Convoy, Murmansk

By W.A. Senovitz

ISBN: 978-1-4669-8803-3 (sc)
ISBN: 978-1-4669-8802-6 (e)

Trafford rev. 07/17/2013

 www.trafford.com

North America & international
toll-free: 1 888 232 4444 (USA & Canada)
fax: 812 355 4082

About the author

I don't know why I waited so long to write this book. I suppose it was because I was working and raising three kids. I also have two great kids from my first marriage. I am 77 years old and I live in a suburb south of Chicago. My wife Karen and I have been married for 48 years. I bowl twice a week, and I also play golf. I should say, "try".

If nothing else, this book will help my kids understand what their grandfather did in world war two. After all, he was part of the greatest generation.

I hope that you enjoy the book.

W. A. Senovitz

FORWARD

This is the true story of my father's experiences in World War II. I know that he didn't think of himself as a hero, he was never awarded any medals for bravery. He was just doing his job. He was in the United States Navy. The official title for his unit was, 'Detached Naval Armed Guard Aboard Merchant Vessels.' When he came home on leave, he rarely said anything about the war. When he did, my brother and I would hang on every word. One time he mentioned going to Murmansk, Russia in a convoy and seeing many dead, frozen bodies on shore. He could see Russian and German uniforms on the bodies. I was in awe, I couldn't wait to go to school the next day to tell the kids in my class. I was so proud of him. We didn't hear many stories about the war. I would ask him all kinds of questions, like, what countries did he go to?. Did he see any action? I didn't get many straight answers. I finally decided that he didn't want to talk about what he had been through. So, most of this story was gleaned from his military record. Anyway, this is what happened in the North Atlantic in 1942.

I believe this is the way he would have told his story.

All of the photos, with the exception of the photos of the S.S. Seattle Spirit and the S.S. Steel Navigator, were taken prior to world war II.

My father, when he was serving on the U.S.S. Richmond.
Sometime around 1923, 1924

1

Every day my Dad would ask me, "Did you find a job yet?". I would have to tell him, "no Pa, not yet" There were plenty of jobs out there, but not what I wanted. I've been out of school about three months. I knew my Dad was getting worried. What really made me look bad, was the fact that my two older sisters and my older brother, all found jobs right away. My brother is an apprentice carpenter. That really made points with my Dad, because he is a cabinet maker. In the old country, he was considered one of the best. My Parents came to America from Hungary. All my life, I had heard the story about my Dad being commissioned by the Kaiser of Germany. When he was given the plans for what he was supposed to build, Pa told them that was not the way to build it. The Germans wouldn't change the plan. Pa told them, to build it their way, would not result in a quality job. So he refused the job. I asked my Dad many times if this story was true, but he never would give me a simple yes or no. My Dad's entire life is based on hard work and quality. Believe me, he is very stubborn and very set in his ways. I think the story is probably true. I can see him doing that.

My Mother's parents raised horses for the Hungarian Army. I guess they were pretty well off. She had a brother that was a Lieutenant in the Army. When he was fighting in some war that Hungary was involved in, he lost an arm in battle. After he died, his artificial arm was placed in a Budapest museum. I believe it is still there.

One day when my Dad came home from work and asked me the usual question, I surprised him. I told him that I had joined the Navy. After he got over the shock, he got a big smile on his face. Right then I knew that I had made the right choice.

My Mother, on the other hand was not very happy. She was worried about my safety and if I would get enough to eat. I assured her that since we were not at war, I would not be in any danger. I also said that I'm sure that I wouldn't eat as well, but I won't starve. That seemed to satisfy her. The following week I left for basic training.

2.

Basic training wasn't as bad as I thought it would be. After we completed the training, we got a well deserved leave. So, all the of gang decided to celebrate. We went into town and drank all night. Boy did we ever get stoned. I woke up in my own bed the next morning and discovered that I had three tattoos. I don't remember how or where, but there they are. I guess I had a good time.

Now we had to wait for our orders. Of course everyone wanted to be assigned to a battleship or at least a destroyer. When I read my orders, I couldn't help myself, I let out a loud yell. I was going to serve aboard the U.S.S. Richmond. She was a new Omaha class, light cruiser. She was commissioned only a few weeks ago. I was the only guy in our group assigned to her. All my buddies could say was "you lucky bastard". I had to report in four days, so I had time to head home to see my folks.

When I walked through the door at home, my Mom hugged me and started to cry. My Dad just got home from work. He was grinning from ear to ear as he shook my hand and also hugged me. It was great to be home. Of course, the first thing my Mom said was, "sit down, I'll fix you something to eat". There was always something cooking on her stove. I sat down and began to enjoy my Mom's cooking. I really missed my Mom's cooking.

After a couple of days of stuffing myself and just relaxing, it was time to head to the Brooklyn Navy Yard and board the Richmond. I didn't want to leave home, but I was really anxious to see my new home. As my Dad walked me to the door, he asked me about my tattoos. I was hoping that he wouldn't notice. I said "I have a couple, it is a Navy tradition". He glared at me as I waited for the avalanche of Hungarian cuss words. Most of which could not be translated into English. I firmly believe that my Father invented most of them. They were very effective. I was totally shocked when all I heard him say was, "tattoos are forever". It would be many years later for me to really understand what he was telling me. I was out walking one warm summer day, when a woman and her little boy passed me going in the opposite direction. The boy turned

U.S.S. Richmond

The U.S.S. Richmond tendered the needs of the United States planes that were in the "Around the World Flight".

U.S.S. Richmond seaplane

U.S.S. Richmond seaplane being lifted onboard.

to look at me and asked his Mother, "Mommy, why are that man's arms painted?". That was the last day I ever wore a short sleeved shirt. Even on the hottest summer days. Now I understood "tattoos are forever".

It was wonderful to see the family again, but I am finally going up the gangplank of the U.S.S. Richmond with my seabag. The year is 1921, I'm twenty years old and I an ready to start my new life in the Navy.

Since the Richmond was a new ship and the crew was mostly inexperienced, we were given daily drills and exercises to train us how to properly run the ship. Then we took her out for her shakedown cruise. As we cut through the sea at speeds of up to 34 knots, I got to know her and love her. She had twelve six inch guns, eight fifty and eight thirty cal. machine guns. After Europe, we went to South America and Africa. She ran like a fine watch. A great ship.

During the next three years, we participated in fleet problems and other exercises. Then we got the call to rescue survivors of a wrecked gunboat. The U.S.S. Tacoma ran aground off the coast of Vera Cruz, Mexico. As we got closer, we could see that she was way up on the rocks. We picked up the crew in lifeboats. That's when we found out that the Captain and the First Officer had drowned trying to get the Tacoma off the rocks. It was a sad ending to a fine ship. The Tacoma and the Richmond had been dispatched to the East Coast of Mexico to protect American interests. There was much unrest, riots, shootings and even some buildings were bombed. But, we did our job and all American interests survived.

Our next assignment was to support the U.S. Army Aviators in the Around the World Flight. Six Countries entered sea planes in a race around the World. The United States entered four planes, two of those were the only planes to finish the race. One of the planes crashed and remaining one broke down.

In 1925 we cruised to Australia, and New Zealand, in 1927 we were

This is the insignia that was on the four planes that the United States entered in the "Around the World Flight" in 1924. The planes were the "Chicago", the "Boston", the "New Orleans" and the "Seattle". Six countries entered the race. The United States, Britain, Argentina, France, Italy and Portugal. Only the United States had planes that finished the grueling race. The "Chicago" and the "New Orleans". The "Seattle" crashed and the "Boston" capsized while being towed.

The "New Orleans

The "Boston", being towed.

Trying to save the "Boston"

The U.S.S. Tacoma, on the rocks at Vera Cruz, Mexico. Jan. 1924

View from deck of U.S.S. Tacoma. Wrecked Jan. 16, 1924

deployed off the coast of China. After the Richmond's Asiatic tour, I decided to take my discharge and try civilian life.

I was lucky, I met a great gal who could cook almost as good as my Mom. We got married, rented a nice apartment and in 1928, we had our first kid, A boy, I was working, making a decent living, we were very happy. In 1929, everything crashed. The stock market, the economy and of course, jobs disappeared. We were like most families in America, struggling to live. It got to a point where I found myself walking along railroad tracks to pick up coal that fell off coal cars when they bumped. We had to have heat. The only one in our family that was working was my younger brother. Fortunately, he ran a bookie joint for one of Chicago's mobsters. He helped us when he could. Somehow we got through the worst days. Then in 1935, we had our second baby boy, I was working most of the time now, so we were getting along pretty well. December 7, 1941 changed everything. Two days later, on December 9th, I enlisted in the Navy. My wife, of course, was furious. I knew that my folks would take care of her and the boys, and she would get most of my Navy pay. So I did what I had to do, enlist. I was forty years old. I wasn't certain that the Navy would take an old man, so I told the recruiter that I was only thirty six. I passed my physical and was on my way to basic training. I think the Navy would have accepted me even if I was in a wheelchair. They desperately needed men with previous military experience. After basic, we started training on 30 cal. And 50 cal. machine guns. We got to be pretty good, at least we could hit the targets. I am sure that I'm the oldest guy in the group. The kids all call me Pops, or Gramps. That's ok, I'll get used to it. All I can say is, these young guys learn fast. After the machine guns, we trained on firing four and five inch deck guns. Everybody began wondering where the training would take us. On the last day, we found out. We were in the auditorium when the Commanding Officer came out to the podium. He told us that because the German submarines were sinking our convoys, particularly in the North Atlantic. The Navy was forming a new unit. We would be part of that unit. We are to be "Detached Naval Armed Guard Aboard Merchant Vessels." Everyone stood up and cheered.

The "old man" told us to shut up and sit down. Then he finished with all of the details. My immediate thought was, "how do we stop a torpedo with guns?" It wasn't going to take long to find out. In less than two weeks, I and the rest of my gun crew were carrying our bags up the gang plank of a freighter which was part of a convoy heading to Murmansk, Russia. Murmansk, I discovered is North of the Artic Circle. When we stepped on board, the freighter crew let out a big cheer. That made us feel welcome. The guys were great. They showed us our bunks and where to stow our gear.

I was Captain of the gun crew, so I was anxious to see the deck gun. We had heard stories that because of a shortage of deck guns, that antique world war one guns were mounted on some ships. I was relieved to see that ours was a newer model. We pulled out of the harbor with about ten merchant ships and two destroyers. We would stop at Reykjavik, Iceland to meet and form the rest of the convoy, about sixty ships and many destroyers. I hope everyone packed their long johns. It looks like its going to be a long, cold trip.

All of our ships docked in the harbor at Reykjavik. Before we went ashore, we were told that most of the other ships in the convoy would arrive some time tomorrow afternoon. That would give us a chance to see the city. The name Iceland tends to give me the shivers, but the weather wasn't that bad. Some of the guys in the crew said that Greenland was colder than Iceland. It's like the names got placed on the wrong countries. We checked out the city. It is a very nice place, the people were friendly, we found what we were looking for, a nice loud bar. All of the guys were thinking what I was thinking, the last part of our trip could be very dangerous. We were hoping the music and beer will help us relax. Because of the rough seas on the trip here, most of the Navy kids were still a little sick, so we only had three or four drinks. We went back to the ship to wait for the rest of the convoy to get here. Late in the afternoon, we left port to form the convoy. All of the ships had previously been assigned positions, so they all maneuvered to their correct place. It is something to see, forty or fifty ships spread out as far as you can see. There must be about a half-mile circle of space between each ship. The convoy can only go as fast of the slowest ship and some of them are very slow. I almost expected to see oars sticking out of a couple of them, but, we plodded along toward Murmansk. The North Atlantic, as usual, was rough. Strong winds and big waves. Some of the kids were throwing up again. Normally, I would be laughing my ass off, but there was too much to be concerned about. We all had heard about the German U-Boat wolf packs sinking hundreds of ships. We were now in their operating area. Everyone was tense and alert (except when they are puking). The first morning out, we were just finishing chow, the loudspeaker blared, "general quarters, general quarters, man your battle stations, enemy aircraft approaching." Everyone scrambled to their battle stations. This freighter had a 4 inch deck gun, two 30 cal. and two 50 cal. machine guns. We saw the planes on our port side. It was a flight of German dive bombers, Stukas. I was scared of course, but what really gets your attention is the sound of their engines when they are diving at your ship. They sound as if they are screaming, a very high pitched scream. Then they drop their bombs. All of the ships in the convoy are firing at them. A couple of ships are now on fire from bomb hits. All hell is breaking loose. The planes are coming around now to strafe us, I can see the flash of his guns. I screamed at one of the guys to get down, but it was too late. He almost got cut in half. Now it was my turn to get sick. Somebody hit one of the planes, I hope it was us. We watched it hit the water. It broke into a thousand pieces. Everyone cheered. The planes finally turned and went back to their base, probably in Norway. We started to look around to see if anyone else had been hit. The merchant crew had two wounded, not real serious, thankfully. The Navy had one killed, he was only twenty years old. A good guy, we will miss him. I don't know if anybody got hit on any of the other ships, I hope not.

Well, if anybody was wondering if the Germans knew where we are, that should answer their question. We all braced for a torpedo attack.

The two ships that got hit by bombs, are now blazing infernos. One was a tanker, probably loaded with aviation fuel, I hope everyone got off in time. Of course, if you are in the water and not in a lifeboat, you will freeze to death in about four minutes.

There is a relatively narrow channel that you have to go through to get into the harbor at Murmansk. As we were going through, I couldn't help thinking what would happen if the Nazi planes came back and caught us in this channel. With no room to maneuver, we could be sitting ducks. Those nasty thoughts quickly vanished as something on shore caught my eye. There were bodies. Hundreds and hundreds of bodies. All frozen. They were stacked like cordwood. I was close enough to see their uniforms. Mostly Russian infantry, but I could see some German uniforms as well. The Russians are probably waiting for a thaw before they can bury them. The frost must go down pretty deep north of the Artic Circle. It was an incredible sight that I will never forget. It illustrates the brutality of war.

We finally docked and we went ashore. Believe me, this place is cold. The wind is always blowing. I just can't seem to get warm. I hope they unload us right away so we can get out of here. That was wishful thinking, four weeks later, we are finally leaving Murmansk. The city and the port were bombed almost every day by the Germans. I guess that I am lucky to get out of there alive.

We headed out of the harbor and through the channel. We set a course for Halifax, and hoped like hell that we wouldn't be spotted by a German U-Boat. We had four merchant vessels and two escorts. The sea was rougher than usual. The waves were at least seven or eight feet high. We figured the rough see would make it almost impossible for a torpedo attack. We figured wrong. About two hours out of port, we heard one hell of an explosion. The last ship in our group took a torpedo that blew most of her bow off. The destroyers were racing around dropping depth charges. I hope we can pick up all of the survivors.

The rest of the trip was pretty quiet, except for the time we spotted four Stukas, they didn't bother with us though. I think that they were probably heading home.

8.

Everyone was happy and relieved to dock at Halifax. We probably had a couple of weeks before the next convoy would be formed. At least that was our guess. Nobody tells anybody anything around here, and of course, that's the way it has to be. The Germans would love to know when we leave. So anyway, we knew we had some time to relax. We went into town every night. We had been through a lot, and we had seen things that we wanted to forget. We certainly tried very hard, and I think we accomplished that much, at least for a few days.

Halifax is a nice town, but lets face it, there isn't much of anything to do here. So, when we finally got our orders, all the guys were ready to go.

It was the middle of June, 1942. Everybody thought we were heading to Russia, but as usual, we guessed wrong. We never get the word until we are under way. It was explained that the fewer people that have this information, the better the chance that it won't leak to the Germans. We don't need a couple of U-boats waiting to ambush us. Actually, we are on our way back to the States. That made the crew and the Guard very happy. New York was probably the best port in the world to have a good time.

When we docked in New York, we were ready for some shore leave. That's when we got the bad news. The crew was going on shore, but the Navy Guard was going to transfer to a ship about to leave port. The S.S. Seattle Spirit (Seas Shipping Co., New York) would be our home for the next week or so. Yes, we were going back to Murmansk. That was probably the last place on Earth that I wanted to see again. Of course, what we were really concerned about was the Nazi subs. We call that area U-boat heaven. Their heaven, our hell. But seeing as how we only work here, no one asked for our opinion.

While we were standing around waiting to board, I noticed the bow of our ship looked different. I couldn't figure it out, so I asked one of the ships officers. He said that any ship going that far North has to have its

SS Seattle Spirit Sunk 18 June 1942

S.S. Seattle Spirit [Seas Shipping Co. Inc., New York] sunk by U-124.
 Four killed, fifty-one survivors

bow reinforced. If we didn't do that, the bow could be crushed if the ship hit an ice floe. He also told me that they place heat coils in all of the water tanks to keep the water from freezing. You learn something new every day.

As we steamed out of the harbor, past the Statue of Liberty, I couldn't help wondering how long it would be before I saw her again. Maybe never. I try not to think about it, but my number could be up anytime. In the middle of June, I felt a cold chill, but that was probably from thinking about going back to Murmansk.

We reached Iceland, but we had to wait three days for the rest of the ships in the convoy to arrive. We finally steamed out the harbor to take our position. We were in station #112. I know I've seen it before, but it is awesome, forty or fifty ships spread out for miles over the ocean is one hell of a sight. I don't know how many escort vessels we have on the trip, but they sure have a lot of ocean to cover.

We were a couple of days out of Reykjavik when it happened. June 18, one of the sailors let out a yell when he saw the wake, but all you can do is hold on tight. The torpedo slammed into the Seattle Spirit on her port side amidships in the engine room and almost immediately flooded the ship. The boiler exploded killing one officer and two crewmen on duty below. The Captain gave the order to abandon ship. Nine Officers, twenty-eight crewman, eleven Navy Armed Guard and seven Canadian passengers got into three lifeboats. One sailor died of shock and exposure after jumping into the water. We weren't in the lifeboats very long, no more than four hours, but it is long enough to have some nasty thoughts. Suppose no one picks us up, how long can we survive? We tried to stay warm as we watched the last ships in the convoy disappear. The night was settling in and these questions started to loom large in our minds. We finally were picked up by the HMCS Agassiz. She is a Canadian corvette. They are similar to a destroyer, but smaller and slower. At that point, we would been happy to see a garbage barge. The short time we were aboard, the Canadians treated us like royalty. They couldn't do enough for us. They were great. They also entertained us, it was a terrific show. They made three or four runs over the u-boat that sank us and dropped about a dozen depth charges on her. It was spectacular. We would make a run, drop the charges and a few seconds later, the bottom of the ocean seemed to erupt. After a couple of passes, I started to feel sorry for the Germans in the sub. Unfortunately, we didn't hit it and we broke off the attack.

Later, we were transferred to the British rescue ship Perth and headed for Halifax. We got there on June 24th. I found out later, that about four hours after the attack, a British Officer boarded the Seattle Spirit to check the damage. When he decided the ship couldn't be salvaged, a corvette shelled the ship until it sank. The Armed Guard arrived back in the States on July 2, 1942 aboard the U.S.S. Brant. We were then detached to the U.S.N. Rest Center, Pocono Manor Inn, Pocono Manor Pennsylvania, for rest and recreation. Being aboard a ship that is torpedoed is a horrifying experience. Death seems to be hovering over the doomed ship. If you survive, you just figure your number wasn't up. It wasn't your time to go, if I'm lucky, maybe the next torpedo will miss.

At the rest center, we relaxed and took it easy. We enjoyed life for about three weeks and waited for our next assignment. Our orders arrived and our Guard unit boarded the Merchant Vessel S.S. Newton (Charles Strubin & Co. Ltd.) Our tour aboard the Newton (I am happy to say) was uneventful and quiet. We did our routine every day, exercises, test fired the guns, and cleaned them thoroughly It was a boring every day routine, but at least we weren't being bombed by Stukas or hunted by u-boats. It was almost like being on a cruise ship. Almost.

August 17, 1942, we got back to the states and completed Armed Guard duty on board the Newton. I took my leave and headed home to see my family. We were living on the far South side of Chicago, renting a pretty nice house. It was set back on a large lot. The house in front had been torn down, and the large excavation hole, littered with rocks and debris was still there. The second day home, the wife and I decided to go a movie. We told the boys, Chuck and the youngest Billy, especially Billy, not to play by that hole. We told them that it was very dangerous. We left Chuck in charge and went out to have a good time at the show. When my wife and I got home, our happy mood quickly changed. There was our youngest son sitting on the couch with a bandage around his head, and a big spot of blood on the right side. Of course, he had to play by that hole and he fell in and hit his head on a rock. We were very mad at first, but then we realized that he could have been killed. Chuck wrapped Billy's head as best he could. Actually, he did a pretty good job. The next day we went to see a doctor. We didn't have a family doctor, so we had to find one in the phone book. We picked one that was in the neighborhood. He actually looked a lot like a current movie star, unfortunately, his medical skills didn't match his looks. He only put two stitches in the wound and after only two days, the stitches broke and the cut got infected. Someone told my wife to keep putting hydrogen peroxide on the cut to kill the infection. That did the job. The cut healed very nicely. We didn't even consider going back to that doctor.

It occurred to me that I had seen more action at home for three days than the entire tour aboard the S.S. Newton. My son's injury wasn't serious so, for the rest of my leave, I had a great time with my family.

Now its time to get back to the war. The year 1942. The war is raging all over the world. Our last convoy landed us in Liverpool. We have been waiting for almost two weeks for our next assignment. Believe me, I'm not hero, but sitting around and waiting is not my thing. All of the guys in my unit feel the same way.

The morning our sailing orders arrived, a big cheer shattered the sullen mood. The number one question on everyone's mind was "where are we going?" The Commanding Officer answered that question, "you guys are heading to New York City on the S.S. Steel Navigator" (Isthmian Lines, U.S.). "Get your gear together, you sail first thing in the morning". We couldn't believe our luck, heading back home. We packed our gear, cleaned up the place and waited for the truck to take us to the dock.

When we got there, we could see that the crew was already on board. The ship had a full cargo, two thousand tons of sand ballast. A couple of the guys from the crew showed us our bunks, it was almost midnight by the time we got our gear stowed. But we had to check the guns and be sure they had enough ammo on board. I don't want to be out in the middle of the ocean and find out that someone forgot to load ammo for the guns. I know that some of the kids in my unit think I'm too careful, but better too careful than dead. Speaking of the kids, I call them kids for a reason, the oldest one just turned twenty. The next oldest is nineteen. The rest of them are eighteen and younger. Considering my age, they are kids. But, they know what is expected of them. They demonstrated that on the practice range. At least that's what I hear.

I really liked what I saw when we checked the guns on this ship. She has a 5 in. Deck gun and four 20 mm. guns placed for and aft, in the right places. I like the 20 mm. It will tear up anything it hits. Lot of fire power. Plenty of ammunition had been loaded on board, just as the man said. But, I feel better now that I've seen it.

I was beat. I hit the crib and dreamt about going home.

The muffled roar of the engines woke me out of a sound sleep. The ship was moving, we were on our way home. It was just beginning to get light in the harbor. I woke up the rest of the Guard crew. We showered, shaved, dressed and made our way to the mess hall. We had a very good breakfast. The chow was pretty good and that was very important. It's a lot easier to keep up the moral if the guys are eating good meals.

I assigned three sailors to each 20mm. and myself and three remaining guys to the 5 in. deck gun. We then went topside to get ammo and store it in a case near the guns. I figured five rounds for the deck gun would be a good start. As soon as we get far enough out of the harbor, we would test fire each weapon.

We watched as the city of Liverpool slowly faded. It was Oct. 9, 1942.

Our ship, the S.S. Steel Navigator was part of a 36 ship convoy, On-137 heading for New York City with a cargo of 2,000 tons of sand ballast. The ships Captains were maneuvering to get to the position that they were assigned. When the convoy was formed, we headed for America. I spotted two Canadian Corvettes, but I'm not sure how many escort vessels are with us. All I can say is, the more the merrier. We're not going to Murmansk this trip, but it only takes one u-boat to make my life miserable. I got permission from the Captain and we test fired each gun. I felt better, the kids were young, but they knew what they were doing. The Navy trained them well. The kids call me gramps, I don't mind, as long as they do their job. They certainly look capable.

The convoy can only go as fast as its slowest ship. I don't think we hit ten knots yet, it was a slow pace, but a steady one. Seven days out and no incidents. Decent weather and no subs. However, October 17th, we found ourselves in the middle of the thickest fog that I have ever seen. I extended my arm and I could not see the tips of my fingers. The Captain must have been as nervous as I was, because he made an announcement that we were going to leave the convoy. He was afraid of colliding with other ships. Our position in the convoy was at the starboard edge, so all he had to do was make a right turn to get clear of other ships. I can understand why the Captain left the convoy, without radar in this thick fog, you don't know what you are going to run into. But now we are on our own. No escort vessels, no protection.

Our situation, however, didn't get any better, we ran into a raging storm. For two days the S.S. Steel Navigator was tossed around the ocean. I don't know how we stayed afloat. I think that the skill of the Master that was steering the ship probably saved our lives. Great seamanship. The power of the storm was so strong, that it caused our cargo to shift. The ship was listing at about 40 degrees. I don't know why we didn't go to the bottom, but we stayed afloat. Thank god. No one would have survived in a lifeboat in this storm.

The Merchant and the Navy gun crew, both volunteered to shift the

Steel Navigator

S.S. Steel Navigator [Isthmian SS Co., New York]. Sunk by U-610 on October 19, 1942. Thirty six dead, sixteen survivors.

cargo by hand. We worked down in the hold for two days. By the third day, we got the list down to 12 degrees (we would later receive a unit citation for our efforts, but all we were trying to do was stay alive). Everybody was totally exhausted. As I mentioned before, our luck wasn't getting any better. At 7:30 a.m. of October 19th, 1942, the third mate sighted a periscope about 400 yards off the starboard beam. The general alarm sounded and the Master turned the ship so the submarine lay astern. The gun crew ran to the stern mounted five inch gun and got off two rounds before the sub went deep. I knew that it was only a matter of time before we would catch a torpedo, we were a ripe target, all alone with no escort. I was hoping that he would surface to finish us off, but the Nazi knew that we had a deck gun that could sink him. At 1:38 p.m. somewhere off Cape Farewell, while steaming at the ten or eleven knots, a torpedo struck between the #1 and #2 holds. The vessel settled by the head and began to sink. The Master immediately ordered the twenty-eight crewmen, eight Officers and sixteen Navy personnel to abandon ship. The motor boat was swamped by the heavy seas. The #3 boat capsized and spilled thirty-five men into the water. Eighteen of them managed to climb onto a raft. The #2 lifeboat cleared the ship and picked up several survivors from the water. To our amazement, the u-boat surfaced about a hundred or so yards from us. It was the U-610. The sub Captain went up to the conning tower, followed by a young crew member carrying a machine gun. We had heard stories of survivors being machine gunned by u-boat crews, so we weren't sure what was going to happen. I thought we were dead.

The young Nazi mounted the gun, swung it around at us and cocked it. The u-boat Captain spoke very good English. He wanted to know what our cargo was, and where is the rest of the convoy? One of the merchant seamen told the u-boat Captain that he should do something sexual to himself. (not his exact words). Personally, I thought his timing was really bad. The nervous kid on the machine gun must have understood what was said to the Captain. I thought he was going to open up on us. We heard the sub Captain shout at him, "nein, nein". The guy on the gun relaxed, and so did I. Finally, he must have decided that he wasn't going to get any answers. The Captain told us to enjoy our trip. He had a smirk on his face that I wished I could erase with my fist. He waved to us as he went below. He was a real cocky s.o.b.. We watched the u-boat disappear into the sea. We were now alone in the middle of the Atlantic Ocean.

Later that night, I don't know how, but some of the guys turned over the #3 boat that was capsized. We had 17 men in the #3 boat and 10 men in the #2 boat. We tried to stay together, but with the storm still raging, we eventually got separated.

We spent the first night just trying to stay afloat. The storm tossed us around like a cork. Everyone was soaking wet. Morning finally arrived and the storm passed. One of the Officers in the boat had a pair of binoculars. He looked in every direction, but he couldn't find the #2 boat. We never saw those guys again. I hd some good friends in the lifeboat.

We spent a good part of the day taking stock of our supplies and trying to get warm. We had several cans of water and some rations. The officers decided that to extend our food and water, only a certain amount will be doled out to each man every day. Hopefully, we will be picked up soon, we pray to God, very soon. One thing became very obvious, there weren't any atheists on board.

The days went by, I lost track. I think this must be day 6 or 7. We are all slowly freezing to death. I can't feel my feet anymore, my hands are also numb. Everyone is in bad shape. I think the end is near. Maybe it would have been better if the Nazi on the sub would have opened up with the machine gun. At least it would have been quick.

We don't have any water or rations left. The wind is picking up again, it is brutal. I think that some of the guys might be dead. I haven't seen anyone move in a long time. It gets worse at night, its even colder. We stay huddled together to stay alive, but is no use, the sea is winning. We have been in this lifeboat at least a week. I don't think we can last much longer. Then we heard the plane, a couple of the men waved, but most of us couldn't move. The Officer with the glasses checked the plane. He said it was pretty high, he didn't think he saw us. Another day went by, no food, no water. Someone said that there was a ship on the horizon. We saw the smoke from her stacks, we watched as she came closer. Finally we could see that she was a destroyer, a British destroyer. The H.M.S. Decoy, she flashed some lights. She was coming for us. Thank God. She pulled up along side to assess our condition. We were in bad shape. It took hours to transfer all of us to the Decoy. One of the freighters crew was dead. I don't know how any of us survived. A total of six Officers, twenty crewmen from the S.S. Steel Navigator and ten U.S. Navy Armed Guard paid with their lives. The date, October 26, 1942. A day that I will never forget. A memorial has been placed in San Pedro, California, honoring the merchant seamen lost on the Steel Navigator.

I have never been so cold in my entire life. The crew on the Decoy made us as comfortable as they could. The hot food was great, but my feet hurt like hell. I tried to walk, but I can't feel my toes. I guess I'm too weak anyway. I looked at my feet and I sure didn't like what I saw. All of them are black at the base. I'm really worried. The medic on the Decoy says I'll by ok, but I'm not so sure. I hope he's right.

They told us that we heading for Gourock, that's a port in Scotland. They say they have a very good hospital there. As I look around at the other guys that were in the lifeboat with me, I think they are in worse condition than I am. I hope everyone makes it. The Brits are doing everything they can for us, they are great.

We docked at Gourock and they started carrying us down the gangplank in stretchers. Just as they got me down to the ambulance, a couple of planes roared by overhead. I guess that I must have looked scared because one of the sailors carrying me said, "don't worry mate, those are ours, they're Spitfires." I have never seen a Spitfire before, but I was happy to see those. I guess the time we got attacked by the German dive bombers rattled my nerves.

We got checked into the hospital and I think we got the best care in the world. The did all kinds of tests on me and about the third day, a doctor came to me and said, "I'm sorry, but I have some bad news. We think that we are going to have to amputate all of your toes, they were damaged pretty badly by the cold. You have very little circulation in them". His words stunned me, it was like getting hit in the face by an oar. I replied, "Doc, you and the nurses here have been great, but nobody is going to cut my toes off." He explained that I could have many problems with them in years to come and that I will be in a lot of pain in cold weather. I again said, "my toes stay". He said that he understands and they will try to save my toes.

The doctors did what they could, and I still have all of my toes. I spent three weeks at Gourock under their excellent care. When I was well enough to leave, I boarded the Queen Elizabeth for the trip to Halifax. Talk about luxury, what a way to travel. She sure is a beautiful ship, but what a prime target for a German sub. We were lucky though, the entire trip was great. We docked on December 10th, and then I got on a train to New York City. I spent a couple of days there until I could catch a train to Chicago. It was wonderful to see my wife and kids again. The doctor was right about pain in cold weather. Every winter my toes hurt like hell, but I still have my toes.

I guess the U.S. Navy didn't need me anymore, or maybe they figured that I was too old. They gave me an honorable discharge in 1943. I know that I'm going to miss the Navy. I guess its in my blood.

The war has been over for about nine years, but I still have dreams. I shouldn't be alive, I should have frozen to death in that lifeboat. In my dream, I can see the smirk on that u-boat captains face that sank my ship. Then, the eight long freezing days and nights in the lifeboat. The cold is so real that I wake up shivering.

But now it is 1954, and I am standing near the Museum of Science and Industry in Chicago. I saw an article in the paper that they were going to place a World War 11 German submarine next to the museum and eventually connect them so that the sub can be toured.

As I watch the workers slowly inch the sub toward its final destination, I can't help wondering if this u-boat was in the "wolf pack " with the sub U-610 that sank my ship. I didn't realize how big they are. I saw the U-610 surface near our lifeboat, but half of it was in the water. I will definitely be back to see what the inside of a u-boat looks like. Lord knows I have seen enough of their outside.

I started thinking about mistakes that I have made in my life and maybe I should have done things differently. But, I did serve my country when she needed every man she could get. Maybe I helped make a difference. I hope so.

Epilog:

My Father died in 1978. On his headstone, after his name and the dates, it says U.S. Navy, World War 11. I think that would have made him feel very proud.   He served his country and helped to defeat our enemies. I certainly am proud of him.

Printed in the United States
By Bookmasters